WEEKLY BUDGET PLANNER
A YEAR-LONG UNDATED SPENDING TRACKER

PETER PAUPER PRESS, INC.
Rye Brook, New York

PETER PAUPER PRESS
Fine Books and Gifts Since 1928

Our Company

In 1928, at the age of twenty-two, Peter Beilenson began printing books on a small press in the basement of his parents' home in Larchmont, New York. Peter—and later, his wife, Edna—sought to create fine books that sold at "prices even a pauper could afford."

Today, still family owned and operated, Peter Pauper Press continues to honor our founders' legacy—and our customers' expectations—of beauty, quality, and value.

Cover images used under license from Shutterstock.com

Designed by Margaret Rubiano

Copyright © 2020 Peter Pauper Press, Inc.
3 International Drive
Rye Brook, NY 10573 USA
All rights reserved
ISBN 978-1-4413-3286-8
Printed in China
14 13 12 11 10

INTRODUCTION

Keep tabs on your money this year with this no-nonsense planner!

Start with the **THINKING AHEAD** section. Write down your **Monthly Income**, then consider your financials for this year. You may wish to use a pencil for this section, so you can erase and revise. Will you have **Major Expenses**, such as replacing your fridge or your car's timing belt? Write them down. What about **Savings**? Are you saving up for a dream bucket list trip? Or do you just want to bump up your savings to cover surprise expenses? Write down your goals here.

Then move on to your first **MONTHLY BUDGET** spread. (You'll find budget pages for all 12 months at the beginning of the book, before the **WEEKLY SPENDING TRACKER** pages.) Project your monthly budget: First, note your monthly income. Then note bills and expenses—things like rent, loan payments, and utilities—along with approximate amounts. Allocate some of what remains to cover necessities like groceries and gas, as well as clothing, entertainment, and savings. Total these estimates to get your target monthly spending and savings.

Next turn to the **WEEKLY SPENDING TRACKER** pages. Write down what you spend each day. Note individual transactions ("coffee," "train fare") or simply note category totals ("food," "transportation"). Tally your total spending at the end of each day, and add up seven days of spending at the end of each week. In the **Notes** section, jot down things like unexpected expenses for that week, whether you're on track with your monthly budget, and so on.

At the end of the year, take stock with **MY YEAR-END SUMMARY**. Total your income, expenses, spending, and savings. How did you do?

At the end of the book, write down **NEXT YEAR'S BUDGET GOALS** and any **NOTES** on your financial journey. And start a new **Weekly Budget Planner**!

THINKING AHEAD

YEAR _____

MONTHLY INCOME	
INCOME SOURCE	TOTAL PER MONTH

TOTAL INCOME PER MONTH _____

MAJOR EXPENSES

Do you foresee major expenses this year? Car repairs? Tuition? New appliances? Plan for those expenses here:

EXPENSE	AMOUNT	TIME FRAME/DUE DATE	TARGET SAVINGS PER MONTH

TOTAL SAVINGS PER MONTH _____

SAVINGS GOALS

Saving for a vacation? A new car? Early retirement? A back-up cushion fund for unplanned expenses that come your way? Write down your goals here:

GOAL	AMOUNT	TIME FRAME/DUE DATE	TARGET SAVINGS PER MONTH
TOTAL SAVINGS PER MONTH			

NOTES

....

....

....

....

....

....

MONTHLY BUDGET

MONTH: _____

INCOME SOURCE	
INCOME SOURCE	
ADDITIONAL INCOME SOURCE	
PROJECTED BUDGET	
PROJECTED SAVINGS	

BILL OR EXPENSE	AMOUNT	DUE DATE	PAID	NOTES
			☐	
			☐	
			☐	
			☐	
			☐	
			☐	
			☐	
			☐	
			☐	
			☐	
			☐	

MONTHLY SUMMARY

SAVINGS THIS MONTH	
TOTAL INCOME THIS MONTH	
TOTAL SPENDING THIS MONTH	

SUNDAY	MONDAY	TUESDAY	WEDNESDAY	THURSDAY	FRIDAY	SATURDAY

MONTHLY BUDGET

MONTH: _____

INCOME SOURCE	
INCOME SOURCE	
ADDITIONAL INCOME SOURCE	
PROJECTED BUDGET	
PROJECTED SAVINGS	

BILL OR EXPENSE	AMOUNT	DUE DATE	PAID	NOTES
			☐	
			☐	
			☐	
			☐	
			☐	
			☐	
			☐	
			☐	
			☐	
			☐	
			☐	

MONTHLY SUMMARY	
SAVINGS THIS MONTH	
TOTAL INCOME THIS MONTH	
TOTAL SPENDING THIS MONTH	

SUNDAY	MONDAY	TUESDAY	WEDNESDAY	THURSDAY	FRIDAY	SATURDAY

MONTHLY BUDGET

MONTH: _____

INCOME SOURCE	
INCOME SOURCE	
ADDITIONAL INCOME SOURCE	
PROJECTED BUDGET	
PROJECTED SAVINGS	

BILL OR EXPENSE	AMOUNT	DUE DATE	PAID	NOTES
			☐	
			☐	
			☐	
			☐	
			☐	
			☐	
			☐	
			☐	
			☐	
			☐	

MONTHLY SUMMARY	
SAVINGS THIS MONTH	
TOTAL INCOME THIS MONTH	
TOTAL SPENDING THIS MONTH	

SUNDAY	MONDAY	TUESDAY	WEDNESDAY	THURSDAY	FRIDAY	SATURDAY

MONTHLY BUDGET

MONTH: _____

INCOME SOURCE	
INCOME SOURCE	
ADDITIONAL INCOME SOURCE	
PROJECTED BUDGET	
PROJECTED SAVINGS	

BILL OR EXPENSE	AMOUNT	DUE DATE	PAID	NOTES
			☐	
			☐	
			☐	
			☐	
			☐	
			☐	
			☐	
			☐	
			☐	
			☐	
			☐	

MONTHLY SUMMARY	
SAVINGS THIS MONTH	
TOTAL INCOME THIS MONTH	
TOTAL SPENDING THIS MONTH	

SUNDAY	MONDAY	TUESDAY	WEDNESDAY	THURSDAY	FRIDAY	SATURDAY

MONTHLY BUDGET

MONTH: _____

INCOME SOURCE	
INCOME SOURCE	
ADDITIONAL INCOME SOURCE	
PROJECTED BUDGET	
PROJECTED SAVINGS	

BILL OR EXPENSE	AMOUNT	DUE DATE	PAID	NOTES
			☐	
			☐	
			☐	
			☐	
			☐	
			☐	
			☐	
			☐	
			☐	
			☐	

MONTHLY SUMMARY	
SAVINGS THIS MONTH	
TOTAL INCOME THIS MONTH	
TOTAL SPENDING THIS MONTH	

SUNDAY	MONDAY	TUESDAY	WEDNESDAY	THURSDAY	FRIDAY	SATURDAY

MONTHLY BUDGET

MONTH: _____

INCOME SOURCE	
INCOME SOURCE	
ADDITIONAL INCOME SOURCE	
PROJECTED BUDGET	
PROJECTED SAVINGS	

BILL OR EXPENSE	AMOUNT	DUE DATE	PAID	NOTES
			☐	
			☐	
			☐	
			☐	
			☐	
			☐	
			☐	
			☐	
			☐	
			☐	
			☐	

MONTHLY SUMMARY

SAVINGS THIS MONTH	
TOTAL INCOME THIS MONTH	
TOTAL SPENDING THIS MONTH	

SUNDAY	MONDAY	TUESDAY	WEDNESDAY	THURSDAY	FRIDAY	SATURDAY

MONTHLY BUDGET

MONTH: _____

INCOME SOURCE	
INCOME SOURCE	
ADDITIONAL INCOME SOURCE	
PROJECTED BUDGET	
PROJECTED SAVINGS	

BILL OR EXPENSE	AMOUNT	DUE DATE	PAID	NOTES
			☐	
			☐	
			☐	
			☐	
			☐	
			☐	
			☐	
			☐	
			☐	
			☐	
			☐	

MONTHLY SUMMARY	
SAVINGS THIS MONTH	
TOTAL INCOME THIS MONTH	
TOTAL SPENDING THIS MONTH	

SUNDAY	MONDAY	TUESDAY	WEDNESDAY	THURSDAY	FRIDAY	SATURDAY

MONTHLY BUDGET

MONTH: _____

INCOME SOURCE	
INCOME SOURCE	
ADDITIONAL INCOME SOURCE	
PROJECTED BUDGET	
PROJECTED SAVINGS	

BILL OR EXPENSE	AMOUNT	DUE DATE	PAID	NOTES
			☐	
			☐	
			☐	
			☐	
			☐	
			☐	
			☐	
			☐	
			☐	
			☐	
			☐	

MONTHLY SUMMARY	
SAVINGS THIS MONTH	
TOTAL INCOME THIS MONTH	
TOTAL SPENDING THIS MONTH	

SUNDAY	MONDAY	TUESDAY	WEDNESDAY	THURSDAY	FRIDAY	SATURDAY

MONTHLY BUDGET

MONTH: _____

INCOME SOURCE	
INCOME SOURCE	
ADDITIONAL INCOME SOURCE	
PROJECTED BUDGET	
PROJECTED SAVINGS	

BILL OR EXPENSE	AMOUNT	DUE DATE	PAID	NOTES
			☐	
			☐	
			☐	
			☐	
			☐	
			☐	
			☐	
			☐	
			☐	
			☐	
			☐	

MONTHLY SUMMARY	
SAVINGS THIS MONTH	
TOTAL INCOME THIS MONTH	
TOTAL SPENDING THIS MONTH	

SUNDAY	MONDAY	TUESDAY	WEDNESDAY	THURSDAY	FRIDAY	SATURDAY

MONTHLY BUDGET

MONTH: _____

INCOME SOURCE	
INCOME SOURCE	
ADDITIONAL INCOME SOURCE	
PROJECTED BUDGET	
PROJECTED SAVINGS	

BILL OR EXPENSE	AMOUNT	DUE DATE	PAID	NOTES
			☐	
			☐	
			☐	
			☐	
			☐	
			☐	
			☐	
			☐	
			☐	
			☐	
			☐	

MONTHLY SUMMARY	
SAVINGS THIS MONTH	
TOTAL INCOME THIS MONTH	
TOTAL SPENDING THIS MONTH	

SUNDAY	MONDAY	TUESDAY	WEDNESDAY	THURSDAY	FRIDAY	SATURDAY

MONTHLY BUDGET

MONTH: _____

INCOME SOURCE	
INCOME SOURCE	
ADDITIONAL INCOME SOURCE	
PROJECTED BUDGET	
PROJECTED SAVINGS	

BILL OR EXPENSE	AMOUNT	DUE DATE	PAID	NOTES
			☐	
			☐	
			☐	
			☐	
			☐	
			☐	
			☐	
			☐	
			☐	
			☐	
			☐	

MONTHLY SUMMARY	
SAVINGS THIS MONTH	
TOTAL INCOME THIS MONTH	
TOTAL SPENDING THIS MONTH	

SUNDAY	MONDAY	TUESDAY	WEDNESDAY	THURSDAY	FRIDAY	SATURDAY

MONTHLY BUDGET

MONTH: _____

INCOME SOURCE	
INCOME SOURCE	
ADDITIONAL INCOME SOURCE	
PROJECTED BUDGET	
PROJECTED SAVINGS	

BILL OR EXPENSE	AMOUNT	DUE DATE	PAID	NOTES
			☐	
			☐	
			☐	
			☐	
			☐	
			☐	
			☐	
			☐	
			☐	
			☐	
			☐	

MONTHLY SUMMARY	
SAVINGS THIS MONTH	
TOTAL INCOME THIS MONTH	
TOTAL SPENDING THIS MONTH	

SUNDAY	MONDAY	TUESDAY	WEDNESDAY	THURSDAY	FRIDAY	SATURDAY

| SUNDAY | MONDAY | TUESDAY | WEDNESDAY | THURSDAY | FRIDAY | SATURDAY |

WEEKLY SPENDING TRACKER

THIS WEEK'S BUDGET _____

WEEK NUMBER 1

_____ to _____
(DATE)   (DATE)

SUNDAY

EXPENSE	AMOUNT
TOTAL:	

MONDAY

EXPENSE	AMOUNT
TOTAL:	

TUESDAY

EXPENSE	AMOUNT
TOTAL:	

WEDNESDAY

EXPENSE	AMOUNT
TOTAL:	

THURSDAY	
EXPENSE	AMOUNT
TOTAL:	

FRIDAY	
EXPENSE	AMOUNT
TOTAL:	

SATURDAY	
EXPENSE	AMOUNT
TOTAL:	

TOTAL SPENDING FOR THE WEEK _____

NOTES

....

....

....

....

....

....

....

....

WEEKLY SPENDING TRACKER

THIS WEEK'S BUDGET _____

WEEK NUMBER 2

_____ to _____
(DATE)   (DATE)

SUNDAY

EXPENSE	AMOUNT
TOTAL:	

MONDAY

EXPENSE	AMOUNT
TOTAL:	

TUESDAY

EXPENSE	AMOUNT
TOTAL:	

WEDNESDAY

EXPENSE	AMOUNT
TOTAL:	

THURSDAY	
EXPENSE	AMOUNT
TOTAL:	

FRIDAY	
EXPENSE	AMOUNT
TOTAL:	

SATURDAY	
EXPENSE	AMOUNT
TOTAL:	

TOTAL SPENDING FOR THE WEEK _____

NOTES

....

....

....

....

....

....

....

WEEKLY SPENDING TRACKER

THIS WEEK'S BUDGET _____

WEEK NUMBER 3

_____ to _____
(DATE)   (DATE)

SUNDAY

EXPENSE	AMOUNT
TOTAL:	

MONDAY

EXPENSE	AMOUNT
TOTAL:	

TUESDAY

EXPENSE	AMOUNT
TOTAL:	

WEDNESDAY

EXPENSE	AMOUNT
TOTAL:	

THURSDAY	
EXPENSE	AMOUNT
TOTAL:	

FRIDAY	
EXPENSE	AMOUNT
TOTAL:	

SATURDAY	
EXPENSE	AMOUNT
TOTAL:	

TOTAL SPENDING FOR THE WEEK _____

NOTES

WEEKLY SPENDING TRACKER

THIS WEEK'S BUDGET _____

WEEK NUMBER 4

_____ to _____
(DATE)   (DATE)

SUNDAY

EXPENSE	AMOUNT
TOTAL:	

MONDAY

EXPENSE	AMOUNT
TOTAL:	

TUESDAY

EXPENSE	AMOUNT
TOTAL:	

WEDNESDAY

EXPENSE	AMOUNT
TOTAL:	

THURSDAY	
EXPENSE	AMOUNT
TOTAL:	

FRIDAY	
EXPENSE	AMOUNT
TOTAL:	

SATURDAY	
EXPENSE	AMOUNT
TOTAL:	

TOTAL SPENDING FOR THE WEEK _____

NOTES

WEEKLY SPENDING TRACKER

THIS WEEK'S BUDGET _____

WEEK NUMBER 5

_____ to _____
(DATE)   (DATE)

SUNDAY	
EXPENSE	AMOUNT
TOTAL:	

MONDAY	
EXPENSE	AMOUNT
TOTAL:	

TUESDAY	
EXPENSE	AMOUNT
TOTAL:	

WEDNESDAY	
EXPENSE	AMOUNT
TOTAL:	

THURSDAY	
EXPENSE	AMOUNT
TOTAL:	

FRIDAY	
EXPENSE	AMOUNT
TOTAL:	

SATURDAY	
EXPENSE	AMOUNT
TOTAL:	

TOTAL SPENDING FOR THE WEEK _____

NOTES

WEEKLY SPENDING TRACKER

THIS WEEK'S BUDGET _____

WEEK NUMBER 6

_____ to _____
(DATE)   (DATE)

SUNDAY

EXPENSE	AMOUNT
	TOTAL:

MONDAY

EXPENSE	AMOUNT
	TOTAL:

TUESDAY

EXPENSE	AMOUNT
	TOTAL:

WEDNESDAY

EXPENSE	AMOUNT
	TOTAL:

THURSDAY	
EXPENSE	AMOUNT
	TOTAL:

FRIDAY	
EXPENSE	AMOUNT
	TOTAL:

SATURDAY	
EXPENSE	AMOUNT
	TOTAL:

TOTAL SPENDING FOR THE WEEK _____

NOTES

....

....

....

....

....

....

....

WEEKLY SPENDING TRACKER

THIS WEEK'S BUDGET _____

WEEK NUMBER 7

_____ to _____
(DATE)   (DATE)

SUNDAY	
EXPENSE	AMOUNT
TOTAL:	

MONDAY	
EXPENSE	AMOUNT
TOTAL:	

TUESDAY	
EXPENSE	AMOUNT
TOTAL:	

WEDNESDAY	
EXPENSE	AMOUNT
TOTAL:	

THURSDAY	
EXPENSE	AMOUNT
TOTAL:	

FRIDAY	
EXPENSE	AMOUNT
TOTAL:	

SATURDAY	
EXPENSE	AMOUNT
TOTAL:	

TOTAL SPENDING FOR THE WEEK _____

NOTES

....

....

....

....

....

....

....

....

WEEKLY SPENDING TRACKER

THIS WEEK'S BUDGET _____

WEEK NUMBER 8

_____ to _____
(DATE)   (DATE)

SUNDAY	
EXPENSE	AMOUNT
TOTAL:	

MONDAY	
EXPENSE	AMOUNT
TOTAL:	

TUESDAY	
EXPENSE	AMOUNT
TOTAL:	

WEDNESDAY	
EXPENSE	AMOUNT
TOTAL:	

THURSDAY	
EXPENSE	AMOUNT
TOTAL:	

FRIDAY	
EXPENSE	AMOUNT
TOTAL:	

SATURDAY	
EXPENSE	AMOUNT
TOTAL:	

TOTAL SPENDING FOR THE WEEK _____

NOTES

....

....

....

....

....

....

....

WEEKLY SPENDING TRACKER

THIS WEEK'S BUDGET _____

WEEK NUMBER 9

_____ to _____
(DATE)   (DATE)

SUNDAY	
EXPENSE	AMOUNT
TOTAL:	

MONDAY	
EXPENSE	AMOUNT
TOTAL:	

TUESDAY	
EXPENSE	AMOUNT
TOTAL:	

WEDNESDAY	
EXPENSE	AMOUNT
TOTAL:	

THURSDAY	
EXPENSE	AMOUNT
TOTAL:	

FRIDAY	
EXPENSE	AMOUNT
TOTAL:	

SATURDAY	
EXPENSE	AMOUNT
TOTAL:	

TOTAL SPENDING FOR THE WEEK _____

NOTES

....

....

....

....

....

....

....

....

WEEKLY SPENDING TRACKER

THIS WEEK'S BUDGET _____

WEEK NUMBER 10

_____ to _____
(DATE)   (DATE)

SUNDAY	
EXPENSE	AMOUNT
TOTAL:	

MONDAY	
EXPENSE	AMOUNT
TOTAL:	

TUESDAY	
EXPENSE	AMOUNT
TOTAL:	

WEDNESDAY	
EXPENSE	AMOUNT
TOTAL:	

THURSDAY	
EXPENSE	AMOUNT
TOTAL:	

FRIDAY	
EXPENSE	AMOUNT
TOTAL:	

SATURDAY	
EXPENSE	AMOUNT
TOTAL:	

TOTAL SPENDING FOR THE WEEK _____

NOTES

WEEKLY SPENDING TRACKER

THIS WEEK'S BUDGET _____

WEEK NUMBER 11

_____ to _____
(DATE)   (DATE)

SUNDAY

EXPENSE	AMOUNT
TOTAL:	

MONDAY

EXPENSE	AMOUNT
TOTAL:	

TUESDAY

EXPENSE	AMOUNT
TOTAL:	

WEDNESDAY

EXPENSE	AMOUNT
TOTAL:	

THURSDAY	
EXPENSE	AMOUNT
TOTAL:	

FRIDAY	
EXPENSE	AMOUNT
TOTAL:	

SATURDAY	
EXPENSE	AMOUNT
TOTAL:	

TOTAL SPENDING FOR THE WEEK _____

NOTES

....

....

....

....

....

....

....

WEEKLY SPENDING TRACKER

THIS WEEK'S BUDGET _____

WEEK NUMBER 12

_____ to _____
(DATE)   (DATE)

SUNDAY

EXPENSE	AMOUNT
	TOTAL:

MONDAY

EXPENSE	AMOUNT
	TOTAL:

TUESDAY

EXPENSE	AMOUNT
	TOTAL:

WEDNESDAY

EXPENSE	AMOUNT
	TOTAL:

THURSDAY	
EXPENSE	AMOUNT
TOTAL:	

FRIDAY	
EXPENSE	AMOUNT
TOTAL:	

SATURDAY	
EXPENSE	AMOUNT
TOTAL:	

TOTAL SPENDING FOR THE WEEK _____

NOTES

....

....

....

....

....

....

....

....

WEEKLY SPENDING TRACKER

WEEK NUMBER 13

THIS WEEK'S BUDGET _____

_____ to _____
(DATE)   (DATE)

SUNDAY

EXPENSE	AMOUNT
TOTAL:	

MONDAY

EXPENSE	AMOUNT
TOTAL:	

TUESDAY

EXPENSE	AMOUNT
TOTAL:	

WEDNESDAY

EXPENSE	AMOUNT
TOTAL:	

THURSDAY	
EXPENSE	AMOUNT
TOTAL:	

FRIDAY	
EXPENSE	AMOUNT
TOTAL:	

SATURDAY	
EXPENSE	AMOUNT
TOTAL:	

TOTAL SPENDING FOR THE WEEK _____

NOTES

....

....

....

....

....

....

....

WEEKLY SPENDING TRACKER

THIS WEEK'S BUDGET _____

WEEK NUMBER 14

_____ to _____
(DATE)   (DATE)

SUNDAY	
EXPENSE	AMOUNT
TOTAL:	

MONDAY	
EXPENSE	AMOUNT
TOTAL:	

TUESDAY	
EXPENSE	AMOUNT
TOTAL:	

WEDNESDAY	
EXPENSE	AMOUNT
TOTAL:	

THURSDAY	
EXPENSE	AMOUNT
TOTAL:	

FRIDAY	
EXPENSE	AMOUNT
TOTAL:	

SATURDAY	
EXPENSE	AMOUNT
TOTAL:	

TOTAL SPENDING FOR THE WEEK _____

NOTES

....

....

....

....

....

....

....

WEEKLY SPENDING TRACKER

THIS WEEK'S BUDGET _____

WEEK NUMBER 15

_____ to _____
(DATE)   (DATE)

SUNDAY	
EXPENSE	AMOUNT
TOTAL:	

MONDAY	
EXPENSE	AMOUNT
TOTAL:	

TUESDAY	
EXPENSE	AMOUNT
TOTAL:	

WEDNESDAY	
EXPENSE	AMOUNT
TOTAL:	

THURSDAY	
EXPENSE	AMOUNT
TOTAL:	

FRIDAY	
EXPENSE	AMOUNT
TOTAL:	

SATURDAY	
EXPENSE	AMOUNT
TOTAL:	

TOTAL SPENDING FOR THE WEEK _____

NOTES

....

....

....

....

....

....

....

WEEKLY SPENDING TRACKER

THIS WEEK'S BUDGET _____

WEEK NUMBER 16

_____ to _____
(DATE)   (DATE)

SUNDAY

EXPENSE	AMOUNT
TOTAL:	

MONDAY

EXPENSE	AMOUNT
TOTAL:	

TUESDAY

EXPENSE	AMOUNT
TOTAL:	

WEDNESDAY

EXPENSE	AMOUNT
TOTAL:	

THURSDAY	
EXPENSE	AMOUNT
TOTAL:	

FRIDAY	
EXPENSE	AMOUNT
TOTAL:	

SATURDAY	
EXPENSE	AMOUNT
TOTAL:	

TOTAL SPENDING FOR THE WEEK _____

NOTES

....

....

....

....

....

....

....

....

WEEKLY SPENDING TRACKER

THIS WEEK'S BUDGET _____

WEEK NUMBER 17

_____ to _____
(DATE)   (DATE)

SUNDAY

EXPENSE	AMOUNT
TOTAL:	

MONDAY

EXPENSE	AMOUNT
TOTAL:	

TUESDAY

EXPENSE	AMOUNT
TOTAL:	

WEDNESDAY

EXPENSE	AMOUNT
TOTAL:	

THURSDAY	
EXPENSE	AMOUNT
TOTAL:	

FRIDAY	
EXPENSE	AMOUNT
TOTAL:	

SATURDAY	
EXPENSE	AMOUNT
TOTAL:	

TOTAL SPENDING FOR THE WEEK _____

NOTES

WEEKLY SPENDING TRACKER

THIS WEEK'S BUDGET _____

WEEK NUMBER 18

_____ to _____
(DATE)   (DATE)

SUNDAY	
EXPENSE	AMOUNT
TOTAL:	

MONDAY	
EXPENSE	AMOUNT
TOTAL:	

TUESDAY	
EXPENSE	AMOUNT
TOTAL:	

WEDNESDAY	
EXPENSE	AMOUNT
TOTAL:	

THURSDAY	
EXPENSE	AMOUNT
TOTAL:	

FRIDAY	
EXPENSE	AMOUNT
TOTAL:	

SATURDAY	
EXPENSE	AMOUNT
TOTAL:	

TOTAL SPENDING FOR THE WEEK _____

NOTES

....

....

....

....

....

....

....

WEEKLY SPENDING TRACKER

WEEK NUMBER 19

THIS WEEK'S BUDGET _____

_____ to _____
(DATE)   (DATE)

SUNDAY

EXPENSE	AMOUNT
	TOTAL:

MONDAY

EXPENSE	AMOUNT
	TOTAL:

TUESDAY

EXPENSE	AMOUNT
	TOTAL:

WEDNESDAY

EXPENSE	AMOUNT
	TOTAL:

THURSDAY	
EXPENSE	AMOUNT
TOTAL:	

FRIDAY	
EXPENSE	AMOUNT
TOTAL:	

SATURDAY	
EXPENSE	AMOUNT
TOTAL:	

TOTAL SPENDING FOR THE WEEK _____

NOTES

....

....

....

....

....

....

....

WEEKLY SPENDING TRACKER

THIS WEEK'S BUDGET _____

WEEK NUMBER 20

_____ to _____
(DATE)   (DATE)

SUNDAY	
EXPENSE	AMOUNT
	TOTAL:

MONDAY	
EXPENSE	AMOUNT
	TOTAL:

TUESDAY	
EXPENSE	AMOUNT
	TOTAL:

WEDNESDAY	
EXPENSE	AMOUNT
	TOTAL:

THURSDAY	
EXPENSE	AMOUNT
TOTAL:	

FRIDAY	
EXPENSE	AMOUNT
TOTAL:	

SATURDAY	
EXPENSE	AMOUNT
TOTAL:	

TOTAL SPENDING FOR THE WEEK _____

NOTES

....

....

....

....

....

....

....

WEEKLY SPENDING TRACKER

THIS WEEK'S BUDGET _____

WEEK NUMBER 21

_____ to _____
(DATE)   (DATE)

SUNDAY

EXPENSE	AMOUNT
TOTAL:	

MONDAY

EXPENSE	AMOUNT
TOTAL:	

TUESDAY

EXPENSE	AMOUNT
TOTAL:	

WEDNESDAY

EXPENSE	AMOUNT
TOTAL:	

THURSDAY	
EXPENSE	AMOUNT
TOTAL:	

FRIDAY	
EXPENSE	AMOUNT
TOTAL:	

SATURDAY	
EXPENSE	AMOUNT
TOTAL:	

TOTAL SPENDING FOR THE WEEK _____

NOTES

....

....

....

....

....

....

....

WEEKLY SPENDING TRACKER

THIS WEEK'S BUDGET _____

WEEK NUMBER 22

_____ to _____
(DATE)   (DATE)

SUNDAY	
EXPENSE	AMOUNT
TOTAL:	

MONDAY	
EXPENSE	AMOUNT
TOTAL:	

TUESDAY	
EXPENSE	AMOUNT
TOTAL:	

WEDNESDAY	
EXPENSE	AMOUNT
TOTAL:	

THURSDAY	
EXPENSE	AMOUNT
	TOTAL:

FRIDAY	
EXPENSE	AMOUNT
	TOTAL:

SATURDAY	
EXPENSE	AMOUNT
	TOTAL:

TOTAL SPENDING FOR THE WEEK _____

NOTES

WEEKLY SPENDING TRACKER

THIS WEEK'S BUDGET _____

WEEK NUMBER 23

_____ to _____
(DATE)   (DATE)

SUNDAY	
EXPENSE	AMOUNT
TOTAL:	

MONDAY	
EXPENSE	AMOUNT
TOTAL:	

TUESDAY	
EXPENSE	AMOUNT
TOTAL:	

WEDNESDAY	
EXPENSE	AMOUNT
TOTAL:	

THURSDAY	
EXPENSE	AMOUNT
TOTAL:	

FRIDAY	
EXPENSE	AMOUNT
TOTAL:	

SATURDAY	
EXPENSE	AMOUNT
TOTAL:	

TOTAL SPENDING FOR THE WEEK _____

NOTES

....
....
....
....
....
....
....

WEEKLY SPENDING TRACKER

THIS WEEK'S BUDGET _____

WEEK NUMBER 24

_____ to _____
(DATE)   (DATE)

SUNDAY

EXPENSE	AMOUNT
TOTAL:	

MONDAY

EXPENSE	AMOUNT
TOTAL:	

TUESDAY

EXPENSE	AMOUNT
TOTAL:	

WEDNESDAY

EXPENSE	AMOUNT
TOTAL:	

THURSDAY	
EXPENSE	AMOUNT
TOTAL:	

FRIDAY	
EXPENSE	AMOUNT
TOTAL:	

SATURDAY	
EXPENSE	AMOUNT
TOTAL:	

TOTAL SPENDING FOR THE WEEK _____

NOTES

....

....

....

....

....

....

....

WEEKLY SPENDING TRACKER

THIS WEEK'S BUDGET _____

WEEK NUMBER 25

_____ to _____
(DATE)   (DATE)

SUNDAY

EXPENSE	AMOUNT
TOTAL:	

MONDAY

EXPENSE	AMOUNT
TOTAL:	

TUESDAY

EXPENSE	AMOUNT
TOTAL:	

WEDNESDAY

EXPENSE	AMOUNT
TOTAL:	

THURSDAY	
EXPENSE	AMOUNT
TOTAL:	

FRIDAY	
EXPENSE	AMOUNT
TOTAL:	

SATURDAY	
EXPENSE	AMOUNT
TOTAL:	

TOTAL SPENDING FOR THE WEEK _____

NOTES

....

....

....

....

....

....

....

WEEKLY SPENDING TRACKER

THIS WEEK'S BUDGET _____

WEEK NUMBER 26

_____ to _____
(DATE)   (DATE)

SUNDAY

EXPENSE	AMOUNT
TOTAL:	

MONDAY

EXPENSE	AMOUNT
TOTAL:	

TUESDAY

EXPENSE	AMOUNT
TOTAL:	

WEDNESDAY

EXPENSE	AMOUNT
TOTAL:	

THURSDAY	
EXPENSE	AMOUNT
TOTAL:	

FRIDAY	
EXPENSE	AMOUNT
TOTAL:	

SATURDAY	
EXPENSE	AMOUNT
TOTAL:	

TOTAL SPENDING FOR THE WEEK _____

NOTES

....

....

....

....

....

....

....

WEEKLY SPENDING TRACKER

THIS WEEK'S BUDGET _____

WEEK NUMBER 27

_____ to _____
(DATE)   (DATE)

SUNDAY

EXPENSE	AMOUNT
TOTAL:	

MONDAY

EXPENSE	AMOUNT
TOTAL:	

TUESDAY

EXPENSE	AMOUNT
TOTAL:	

WEDNESDAY

EXPENSE	AMOUNT
TOTAL:	

THURSDAY	
EXPENSE	AMOUNT
TOTAL:	

FRIDAY	
EXPENSE	AMOUNT
TOTAL:	

SATURDAY	
EXPENSE	AMOUNT
TOTAL:	

TOTAL SPENDING FOR THE WEEK _____

NOTES

....

....

....

....

....

....

....

WEEKLY SPENDING TRACKER

THIS WEEK'S BUDGET _____

WEEK NUMBER 28

_____ to _____
(DATE)   (DATE)

SUNDAY

EXPENSE	AMOUNT
TOTAL:	

MONDAY

EXPENSE	AMOUNT
TOTAL:	

TUESDAY

EXPENSE	AMOUNT
TOTAL:	

WEDNESDAY

EXPENSE	AMOUNT
TOTAL:	

THURSDAY	
EXPENSE	AMOUNT
TOTAL:	

FRIDAY	
EXPENSE	AMOUNT
TOTAL:	

SATURDAY	
EXPENSE	AMOUNT
TOTAL:	

TOTAL SPENDING FOR THE WEEK _____

NOTES

....

....

....

....

....

....

....

WEEKLY SPENDING TRACKER

THIS WEEK'S BUDGET _____

WEEK NUMBER 29

_____ to _____
(DATE)   (DATE)

SUNDAY

EXPENSE	AMOUNT
TOTAL:	

MONDAY

EXPENSE	AMOUNT
TOTAL:	

TUESDAY

EXPENSE	AMOUNT
TOTAL:	

WEDNESDAY

EXPENSE	AMOUNT
TOTAL:	

THURSDAY	
EXPENSE	AMOUNT
TOTAL:	

FRIDAY	
EXPENSE	AMOUNT
TOTAL:	

SATURDAY	
EXPENSE	AMOUNT
TOTAL:	

TOTAL SPENDING FOR THE WEEK _____

NOTES

WEEKLY SPENDING TRACKER

THIS WEEK'S BUDGET _____

WEEK NUMBER 30

_____ to _____
(DATE)   (DATE)

SUNDAY	
EXPENSE	AMOUNT
TOTAL:	

MONDAY	
EXPENSE	AMOUNT
TOTAL:	

TUESDAY	
EXPENSE	AMOUNT
TOTAL:	

WEDNESDAY	
EXPENSE	AMOUNT
TOTAL:	

THURSDAY	
EXPENSE	AMOUNT
TOTAL:	

FRIDAY	
EXPENSE	AMOUNT
TOTAL:	

SATURDAY	
EXPENSE	AMOUNT
TOTAL:	

TOTAL SPENDING FOR THE WEEK _____

NOTES

WEEKLY SPENDING TRACKER

THIS WEEK'S BUDGET _____

WEEK NUMBER 31

_____ to _____
(DATE)   (DATE)

SUNDAY

EXPENSE	AMOUNT
TOTAL:	

MONDAY

EXPENSE	AMOUNT
TOTAL:	

TUESDAY

EXPENSE	AMOUNT
TOTAL:	

WEDNESDAY

EXPENSE	AMOUNT
TOTAL:	

THURSDAY

EXPENSE	AMOUNT
TOTAL:	

FRIDAY

EXPENSE	AMOUNT
TOTAL:	

SATURDAY

EXPENSE	AMOUNT
TOTAL:	

TOTAL SPENDING FOR THE WEEK _____

NOTES

....

....

....

....

....

....

....

....

WEEKLY SPENDING TRACKER

THIS WEEK'S BUDGET _____

WEEK NUMBER 32

_____ to _____
(DATE)   (DATE)

SUNDAY

EXPENSE	AMOUNT
TOTAL:	

MONDAY

EXPENSE	AMOUNT
TOTAL:	

TUESDAY

EXPENSE	AMOUNT
TOTAL:	

WEDNESDAY

EXPENSE	AMOUNT
TOTAL:	

THURSDAY	
EXPENSE	AMOUNT
TOTAL:	

FRIDAY	
EXPENSE	AMOUNT
TOTAL:	

SATURDAY	
EXPENSE	AMOUNT
TOTAL:	

TOTAL SPENDING FOR THE WEEK _____

NOTES

....

....

....

....

....

....

....

....

WEEKLY SPENDING TRACKER

THIS WEEK'S BUDGET _____

WEEK NUMBER 33

_____ to _____
(DATE)   (DATE)

SUNDAY	
EXPENSE	AMOUNT
TOTAL:	

MONDAY	
EXPENSE	AMOUNT
TOTAL:	

TUESDAY	
EXPENSE	AMOUNT
TOTAL:	

WEDNESDAY	
EXPENSE	AMOUNT
TOTAL:	

THURSDAY	
EXPENSE	AMOUNT
	TOTAL:

FRIDAY	
EXPENSE	AMOUNT
	TOTAL:

SATURDAY	
EXPENSE	AMOUNT
	TOTAL:

TOTAL SPENDING FOR THE WEEK _____

NOTES

....

....

....

....

....

....

....

....

WEEKLY SPENDING TRACKER

THIS WEEK'S BUDGET _____

WEEK NUMBER 34

_____ to _____
(DATE)   (DATE)

SUNDAY

EXPENSE	AMOUNT
	TOTAL:

MONDAY

EXPENSE	AMOUNT
	TOTAL:

TUESDAY

EXPENSE	AMOUNT
	TOTAL:

WEDNESDAY

EXPENSE	AMOUNT
	TOTAL:

THURSDAY	
EXPENSE	AMOUNT
TOTAL:	

FRIDAY	
EXPENSE	AMOUNT
TOTAL:	

SATURDAY	
EXPENSE	AMOUNT
TOTAL:	

TOTAL SPENDING FOR THE WEEK _____

NOTES

....

....

....

....

....

....

....

WEEKLY SPENDING TRACKER

THIS WEEK'S BUDGET _____

WEEK NUMBER 35

_____ to _____
(DATE)   (DATE)

SUNDAY

EXPENSE	AMOUNT
TOTAL:	

MONDAY

EXPENSE	AMOUNT
TOTAL:	

TUESDAY

EXPENSE	AMOUNT
TOTAL:	

WEDNESDAY

EXPENSE	AMOUNT
TOTAL:	

THURSDAY	
EXPENSE	AMOUNT
	TOTAL:

FRIDAY	
EXPENSE	AMOUNT
	TOTAL:

SATURDAY	
EXPENSE	AMOUNT
	TOTAL:

TOTAL SPENDING FOR THE WEEK _____

NOTES

....

....

....

....

....

....

....

....

WEEKLY SPENDING TRACKER

THIS WEEK'S BUDGET _____

WEEK NUMBER 36

_____ to _____
(DATE)   (DATE)

SUNDAY

EXPENSE	AMOUNT
TOTAL:	

MONDAY

EXPENSE	AMOUNT
TOTAL:	

TUESDAY

EXPENSE	AMOUNT
TOTAL:	

WEDNESDAY

EXPENSE	AMOUNT
TOTAL:	

THURSDAY	
EXPENSE	AMOUNT
TOTAL:	

FRIDAY	
EXPENSE	AMOUNT
TOTAL:	

SATURDAY	
EXPENSE	AMOUNT
TOTAL:	

TOTAL SPENDING FOR THE WEEK _____

NOTES

....

....

....

....

....

....

....

WEEKLY SPENDING TRACKER

THIS WEEK'S BUDGET _____

WEEK NUMBER 37

_____ to _____
(DATE)   (DATE)

SUNDAY	
EXPENSE	AMOUNT
TOTAL:	

MONDAY	
EXPENSE	AMOUNT
TOTAL:	

TUESDAY	
EXPENSE	AMOUNT
TOTAL:	

WEDNESDAY	
EXPENSE	AMOUNT
TOTAL:	

THURSDAY	
EXPENSE	AMOUNT
	TOTAL:

FRIDAY	
EXPENSE	AMOUNT
	TOTAL:

SATURDAY	
EXPENSE	AMOUNT
	TOTAL:

TOTAL SPENDING FOR THE WEEK _____

NOTES

....

....

....

....

....

....

....

WEEKLY SPENDING TRACKER

THIS WEEK'S BUDGET _____

WEEK NUMBER 38

_____ to _____
(DATE)   (DATE)

SUNDAY

EXPENSE	AMOUNT
	TOTAL:

MONDAY

EXPENSE	AMOUNT
	TOTAL:

TUESDAY

EXPENSE	AMOUNT
	TOTAL:

WEDNESDAY

EXPENSE	AMOUNT
	TOTAL:

THURSDAY	
EXPENSE	AMOUNT
TOTAL:	

FRIDAY	
EXPENSE	AMOUNT
TOTAL:	

SATURDAY	
EXPENSE	AMOUNT
TOTAL:	

TOTAL SPENDING FOR THE WEEK _____

NOTES

....

....

....

....

....

....

....

....

WEEKLY SPENDING TRACKER

THIS WEEK'S BUDGET _____

WEEK NUMBER 39

_____ to _____
(DATE)   (DATE)

SUNDAY

EXPENSE	AMOUNT
TOTAL:	

MONDAY

EXPENSE	AMOUNT
TOTAL:	

TUESDAY

EXPENSE	AMOUNT
TOTAL:	

WEDNESDAY

EXPENSE	AMOUNT
TOTAL:	

THURSDAY	
EXPENSE	AMOUNT
TOTAL:	

FRIDAY	
EXPENSE	AMOUNT
TOTAL:	

SATURDAY	
EXPENSE	AMOUNT
TOTAL:	

TOTAL SPENDING FOR THE WEEK _____

NOTES

....

....

....

....

....

....

....

WEEKLY SPENDING TRACKER

THIS WEEK'S BUDGET _____

WEEK NUMBER 40

_____ to _____
(DATE)   (DATE)

SUNDAY

EXPENSE	AMOUNT
	TOTAL:

MONDAY

EXPENSE	AMOUNT
	TOTAL:

TUESDAY

EXPENSE	AMOUNT
	TOTAL:

WEDNESDAY

EXPENSE	AMOUNT
	TOTAL:

THURSDAY	
EXPENSE	AMOUNT
TOTAL:	

FRIDAY	
EXPENSE	AMOUNT
TOTAL:	

SATURDAY	
EXPENSE	AMOUNT
TOTAL:	

TOTAL SPENDING FOR THE WEEK _____

NOTES

....

....

....

....

....

....

....

WEEKLY SPENDING TRACKER

THIS WEEK'S BUDGET _____

WEEK NUMBER 41

_____ to _____
(DATE)   (DATE)

SUNDAY

EXPENSE	AMOUNT
TOTAL:	

MONDAY

EXPENSE	AMOUNT
TOTAL:	

TUESDAY

EXPENSE	AMOUNT
TOTAL:	

WEDNESDAY

EXPENSE	AMOUNT
TOTAL:	

THURSDAY	
EXPENSE	AMOUNT
TOTAL:	

FRIDAY	
EXPENSE	AMOUNT
TOTAL:	

SATURDAY	
EXPENSE	AMOUNT
TOTAL:	

TOTAL SPENDING FOR THE WEEK _____

NOTES

....

....

....

....

....

....

....

WEEKLY SPENDING TRACKER

WEEK NUMBER 42

THIS WEEK'S BUDGET _____

_____ to _____
(DATE)   (DATE)

SUNDAY	
EXPENSE	AMOUNT
	TOTAL:

MONDAY	
EXPENSE	AMOUNT
	TOTAL:

TUESDAY	
EXPENSE	AMOUNT
	TOTAL:

WEDNESDAY	
EXPENSE	AMOUNT
	TOTAL:

THURSDAY	
EXPENSE	AMOUNT
TOTAL:	

FRIDAY	
EXPENSE	AMOUNT
TOTAL:	

SATURDAY	
EXPENSE	AMOUNT
TOTAL:	

TOTAL SPENDING FOR THE WEEK _____

NOTES

....

....

....

....

....

....

....

WEEKLY SPENDING TRACKER

THIS WEEK'S BUDGET _____

WEEK NUMBER 43

_____ to _____
(DATE)   (DATE)

SUNDAY	
EXPENSE	AMOUNT
TOTAL:	

MONDAY	
EXPENSE	AMOUNT
TOTAL:	

TUESDAY	
EXPENSE	AMOUNT
TOTAL:	

WEDNESDAY	
EXPENSE	AMOUNT
TOTAL:	

THURSDAY	
EXPENSE	AMOUNT
TOTAL:	

FRIDAY	
EXPENSE	AMOUNT
TOTAL:	

SATURDAY	
EXPENSE	AMOUNT
TOTAL:	

TOTAL SPENDING FOR THE WEEK _____

NOTES

....

....

....

....

....

....

....

WEEKLY SPENDING TRACKER

THIS WEEK'S BUDGET _____

WEEK NUMBER 44

_____ to _____
(DATE)   (DATE)

SUNDAY

EXPENSE	AMOUNT
TOTAL:	

MONDAY

EXPENSE	AMOUNT
TOTAL:	

TUESDAY

EXPENSE	AMOUNT
TOTAL:	

WEDNESDAY

EXPENSE	AMOUNT
TOTAL:	

THURSDAY	
EXPENSE	AMOUNT
TOTAL:	

FRIDAY	
EXPENSE	AMOUNT
TOTAL:	

SATURDAY	
EXPENSE	AMOUNT
TOTAL:	

TOTAL SPENDING FOR THE WEEK _____

NOTES

....

....

....

....

....

....

....

WEEKLY SPENDING TRACKER

THIS WEEK'S BUDGET _____

WEEK NUMBER 45

_____ to _____
(DATE)   (DATE)

SUNDAY

EXPENSE	AMOUNT
	TOTAL:

MONDAY

EXPENSE	AMOUNT
	TOTAL:

TUESDAY

EXPENSE	AMOUNT
	TOTAL:

WEDNESDAY

EXPENSE	AMOUNT
	TOTAL:

THURSDAY	
EXPENSE	AMOUNT
TOTAL:	

FRIDAY	
EXPENSE	AMOUNT
TOTAL:	

SATURDAY	
EXPENSE	AMOUNT
TOTAL:	

TOTAL SPENDING FOR THE WEEK _____

NOTES

....

....

....

....

....

....

....

WEEKLY SPENDING TRACKER

THIS WEEK'S BUDGET _____

WEEK NUMBER 46

_____ to _____
(DATE)   (DATE)

SUNDAY	
EXPENSE	AMOUNT
TOTAL:	

MONDAY	
EXPENSE	AMOUNT
TOTAL:	

TUESDAY	
EXPENSE	AMOUNT
TOTAL:	

WEDNESDAY	
EXPENSE	AMOUNT
TOTAL:	

THURSDAY	
EXPENSE	AMOUNT
	TOTAL:

FRIDAY	
EXPENSE	AMOUNT
	TOTAL:

SATURDAY	
EXPENSE	AMOUNT
	TOTAL:

TOTAL SPENDING FOR THE WEEK _____

NOTES

....

....

....

....

....

....

....

WEEKLY SPENDING TRACKER

THIS WEEK'S BUDGET _____

WEEK NUMBER 47

_____ to _____
(DATE)   (DATE)

SUNDAY

EXPENSE	AMOUNT
TOTAL:	

MONDAY

EXPENSE	AMOUNT
TOTAL:	

TUESDAY

EXPENSE	AMOUNT
TOTAL:	

WEDNESDAY

EXPENSE	AMOUNT
TOTAL:	

THURSDAY	
EXPENSE	AMOUNT
TOTAL:	

FRIDAY	
EXPENSE	AMOUNT
TOTAL:	

SATURDAY	
EXPENSE	AMOUNT
TOTAL:	

TOTAL SPENDING FOR THE WEEK _____

NOTES

....

....

....

....

....

....

....

WEEKLY SPENDING TRACKER

THIS WEEK'S BUDGET _____

WEEK NUMBER 48

_____ to _____
(DATE)   (DATE)

SUNDAY	
EXPENSE	AMOUNT
TOTAL:	

MONDAY	
EXPENSE	AMOUNT
TOTAL:	

TUESDAY	
EXPENSE	AMOUNT
TOTAL:	

WEDNESDAY	
EXPENSE	AMOUNT
TOTAL:	

THURSDAY	
EXPENSE	AMOUNT
TOTAL:	

FRIDAY	
EXPENSE	AMOUNT
TOTAL:	

SATURDAY	
EXPENSE	AMOUNT
TOTAL:	

TOTAL SPENDING FOR THE WEEK _____

NOTES

....

....

....

....

....

....

....

....

WEEKLY SPENDING TRACKER

THIS WEEK'S BUDGET _____

WEEK NUMBER 49

_____ to _____
(DATE)   (DATE)

SUNDAY	
EXPENSE	AMOUNT
TOTAL:	

MONDAY	
EXPENSE	AMOUNT
TOTAL:	

TUESDAY	
EXPENSE	AMOUNT
TOTAL:	

WEDNESDAY	
EXPENSE	AMOUNT
TOTAL:	

THURSDAY	
EXPENSE	AMOUNT
TOTAL:	

FRIDAY	
EXPENSE	AMOUNT
TOTAL:	

SATURDAY	
EXPENSE	AMOUNT
TOTAL:	

TOTAL SPENDING FOR THE WEEK _____

NOTES

WEEKLY SPENDING TRACKER

THIS WEEK'S BUDGET _____

WEEK NUMBER 50

_____ to _____
(DATE)   (DATE)

SUNDAY	
EXPENSE	AMOUNT
TOTAL:	

MONDAY	
EXPENSE	AMOUNT
TOTAL:	

TUESDAY	
EXPENSE	AMOUNT
TOTAL:	

WEDNESDAY	
EXPENSE	AMOUNT
TOTAL:	

THURSDAY

EXPENSE	AMOUNT
TOTAL:	

FRIDAY

EXPENSE	AMOUNT
TOTAL:	

SATURDAY

EXPENSE	AMOUNT
TOTAL:	

TOTAL SPENDING FOR THE WEEK _____

NOTES

....

....

....

....

....

....

....

WEEKLY SPENDING TRACKER

THIS WEEK'S BUDGET _____

WEEK NUMBER 51

_____ to _____
(DATE)   (DATE)

SUNDAY

EXPENSE	AMOUNT
TOTAL:	

MONDAY

EXPENSE	AMOUNT
TOTAL:	

TUESDAY

EXPENSE	AMOUNT
TOTAL:	

WEDNESDAY

EXPENSE	AMOUNT
TOTAL:	

THURSDAY	
EXPENSE	AMOUNT
	TOTAL:

FRIDAY	
EXPENSE	AMOUNT
	TOTAL:

SATURDAY	
EXPENSE	AMOUNT
	TOTAL:

TOTAL SPENDING FOR THE WEEK _____

NOTES

....

....

....

....

....

....

....

WEEKLY SPENDING TRACKER

THIS WEEK'S BUDGET _____

WEEK NUMBER 52

_____ to _____
(DATE)   (DATE)

SUNDAY	
EXPENSE	AMOUNT
TOTAL:	

MONDAY	
EXPENSE	AMOUNT
TOTAL:	

TUESDAY	
EXPENSE	AMOUNT
TOTAL:	

WEDNESDAY	
EXPENSE	AMOUNT
TOTAL:	

THURSDAY	
EXPENSE	AMOUNT
TOTAL:	

FRIDAY	
EXPENSE	AMOUNT
TOTAL:	

SATURDAY	
EXPENSE	AMOUNT
TOTAL:	

TOTAL SPENDING FOR THE WEEK _____

NOTES

....

....

....

....

....

....

....

WEEKLY SPENDING TRACKER

WEEK NUMBER 53

THIS WEEK'S BUDGET _____

_____ to _____
(DATE)   (DATE)

SUNDAY	
EXPENSE	AMOUNT
TOTAL:	

MONDAY	
EXPENSE	AMOUNT
TOTAL:	

TUESDAY	
EXPENSE	AMOUNT
TOTAL:	

WEDNESDAY	
EXPENSE	AMOUNT
TOTAL:	

THURSDAY	
EXPENSE	AMOUNT
TOTAL:	

FRIDAY	
EXPENSE	AMOUNT
TOTAL:	

SATURDAY	
EXPENSE	AMOUNT
TOTAL:	

TOTAL SPENDING FOR THE WEEK _____

NOTES

....

....

....

....

....

....

....

MY YEAR-END SUMMARY

TOTAL INCOME	
TOTAL SPENDING FOR THE YEAR	
TOTAL SAVINGS FOR THE YEAR	

MONTH 1:
INCOME	
EXPENSES	
SAVINGS	

MONTH 5:
INCOME	
EXPENSES	
SAVINGS	

MONTH 2:
INCOME	
EXPENSES	
SAVINGS	

MONTH 6:
INCOME	
EXPENSES	
SAVINGS	

MONTH 3:
INCOME	
EXPENSES	
SAVINGS	

MONTH 7:
INCOME	
EXPENSES	
SAVINGS	

MONTH 4:
INCOME	
EXPENSES	
SAVINGS	

MONTH 8:
INCOME	
EXPENSES	
SAVINGS	

MONTH 9:	
INCOME	
EXPENSES	
SAVINGS	

MONTH 11:	
INCOME	
EXPENSES	
SAVINGS	

MONTH 10:	
INCOME	
EXPENSES	
SAVINGS	

MONTH 12:	
INCOME	
EXPENSES	
SAVINGS	

NOTES

NEXT YEAR'S BUDGET GOALS

NOTES